Things I Would Never Say in an Interview

POEMS

Julie Grace

Wild Cape Press, LLC

Things I Would Never Say in an Interview

Author's Note

I HAVE FACED many horrors of this world; I do not wish to remind you of yours unless you are looking for some solace in the company of the battered and bruised. If so, I welcome you open-armed; hopefully, we can both find strength and wisdom here. If you do not wish to read further about themes of sexual assault and domestic abuse, then please feel free to put this down and find the joy you need elsewhere.

I wish I could promise you, dear reader, a happy ending, but I cannot. Please do not falter. It is only because any ending, happy or sad, has yet to be written. As much as I wish this story to end happily, I am not optimistic. I know that my story is only a small chapter in a growing tome. If you have a chapter next to mine, I wish you everything that you deserve, especially if you can't picture yourself receiving it.

Hello

"What are you afraid of?"
The inevitable question always responded to with nothing. Nothing seems to satisfy the hungry questioners. They always thought this must be a brave answer. To be afraid of nothing. But the truth is, being afraid of nothing means being afraid of feeling nothing, doing nothing, being nothing. So yes, I am afraid of nothing.

Your Hobbies

"Oh! You're a writer? What do you write?"

~~Broken phrases and crossed-out words.~~

Sparks of Confidence

I have a fire inside me that burns constantly.
Sometimes, it burns me.
Other times, it burns my obstacles.

Either way,
I think I like it.

R & R

You were Romeo,
But I was Rosaline.

You loved love, Lover,
Your sweet words and heavy touches
Convinced so many.

It was said I had your love.
With a heart so inconsistent,
Who knows?

Your changing affections
Resulted in mass confusion.
I hope it haunts you.

I'm glad you found your Juliet.
I'm sure you will both find salvation in your demise.

Confidence

You can whisper and gossip behind my back.
You can say all you want,
But someday I'll rise above this.
Did I upset you?
Why else would you talk?
Because I smile like I've got Aphrodite's touch, to be used at my will.
Did you wish to find my Achilles heel?
To shoot me and laugh at my misfortune?
Curled up in front of Olympus,
Awaiting my judgment.
This is one thing I will not do.
To sanction my victimhood to you.
Yes, Athena taught me well:
Someday I will rise above this.
Does my confidence surprise you?
Don't let me take yours,
Because I walk around like I have the world at my fingertips, to be
formed to my ideal.
Atlas holds the world upon his shoulders, yet I will not ask him to
hold mine.
I will gladly take the burden
Just to say it's mine.
I'll rise above your bitterness,
I'll rise above your lies.
I'll rise someday to your astonishment, yes, someday, I'll rise.

Not Another Feminist Rant

I have never been one for feminist rants.
Never one to preach on a soap box about the woes of the fairer sex.
It was never needed.
The three fates did not need Hades—
Hell, he needed them!
To file and direct the ongoing of his realm,
Not as secretaries, but as the deciding vote.
This is not a feminist rant.
It is just a reminder.
That without Moirea,
There would be no destiny, inevitability, or fortune.
And those are the real Gods we worship today
With their long lists all
Inscribed in iron.
Furies need not for the race of man.
So no, this is not a feminist rant.

Ambition

What makes women ambitious?
What makes them go through hell

For a crown picked off a bloody head?
Don't women know that this is a man's world, and women will die
so that they can keep it?

Women will die with their daughters' names on their lips.
Women will die with a B on their necks.
Women will die holding their sons.
Women will die with insults burned onto their skins.
Women will die thinking of the life they wanted.
Women will die for the sake of man's whims.

So, what makes women ambitious?
So, what makes them go through hell?

Please

All I ever asked for
Was for you to pick up a knife.
Little did I know you would,
Only to bury that knife into me.

All I ever asked for
Was for you to build me a fence.
Little did I know you would,
Only to keep me locked away.

All I ever asked for
Was for you to stay.
Little did I know you would,
Only to stay far away from me.

All I ever asked for
Was for you to leave.
Little did I know you would,
Only to blame me for your journey.

Tap Tap Tapping

I pray that the tap, tap, tapping at my chamber door is friend, not foe. I know that it isn't from the tenacity in the taps. I know it is you. Even as a ghost, your force pins me, stripping away the joys of sweet wine and light in the darkest of places. I am forever destined to hunt for that light, only to find its way blocked.

Athena's Gift

Thrown to a sacred floor,
My beauty stolen,
Replaced by venom:
This is no protection.
We all know
The only true protection
Is an X and Y.
From your hatred
You'll turn to stone.
All I possess now
Is a museum of my abusers.

One Taste

For all the good I try to do, will it make up for all that I have done?
When will wishes wander down their chosen paths,
Far from that which has not been wished away?
I have taken a bite out of the pomegranate,
Crimson dripping down my lips,
Seeds popping against my teeth.

I Know

I know why she took her first step down, and why she stayed. For all good, sweet things take diligence. I, like she, stumbled in. But once inside, we became queens. No, not just queens but something more.

No longer were our lives dictated by the comings and goings of the moon or men. We dictate the coming of growth and happiness. All because of that one step.

Temples

Yes, my body is a temple;
It is a temple for Athena
Next to the sea.
The storms that blow in
Have weathered the altar;
It stands cracked and worn
With blood drops on the steps.
Please be careful,
I don't want you to slip.

Contradictions

It is no small matter to be full of sunshine and flora as well as death
and smoke.
To do so is to hold great power beneath your skin, like thorns
ready to cut. Just remember, the loveliest flowers have the tough-
est thorns.

CHNOPS

I am.
I matter.

But
I could lose this.
I will give in.
I will be a stranger,
Another number;
I will be forgotten.

Never realizing how demoralizing life is,
I can find myself slipping away
As others are forgotten too.
Is the answer for all of us to slip away behind masks of fear and
hate?

Some fight and win, backed by those masks.
I find myself numb, not from drugs or alcohol but from mindless-
ness and idiosyncrasies.
I hide from the cry of my soul. It longs for creative rebirth, and all I
can give it is the same tired words I tell myself over and over again.

I could lose this.
I will give in.
I will be a stranger,
Another number;
I will be forgotten.

Too afraid of what my broken heart will create, I am slowly killing
it. It feels more humane. Muzzling it only to find it has choked on
the repressed thoughts of,
Is a soulless life worth living in comfortable numbness?

No.

I want to matter.
But not just to matter.
To bring forth a new age,
A new age of complete distinctiveness
So complete that everyone must take heed.
And to matter.

Seventeen

I sold my soul at 17.
It was an easy deal.
I traded my inner monologue
for the voice of a devil,
Forever destined to listen to the worst,
Until I learned how to win my demons over.

At 25, we have tea and gossip
about the ones who never learned
the value of finding friendships
within the deals one makes at 17.

Protection

I wear armor every day,
Tattoos on my skin,
Knives hidden in my boots.
What once may have dammed me
Has now saved me.
They tell my story better than I could.

If you are nice,
I'll let you read it.

7 x 7

Back up against the wall,
I feel all of you
All over me.
I would kill to keep this feeling.

I gaze into the mirror;
I see numbers collecting
Over my hips, thighs, and stomach.
Each pound weighs me down.

Looking back into your eyes,
All I see is what you can do for me.
Together we can succeed,
But only if we use each other.

I watch your panic as the door rattles.
Slowly, I pull up the sheets.
I can't be bothered to dress.
Let them see me in my shame.

I see the look you shoot me;
There is no love there.
I reciprocate.
Maybe that's why we are together.

Something catches my eye.
I look over to the ring pinned to the wall;
It doesn't fit me,
But I know it fits her.

Months later I look at my phone.
I see the half-hearted text, "I can't,"
Wishing I sent it first,
But I know what made me stay.

Never

I was not made for forgiveness.
I long for vengeance in my veins.

Each drop of blood spurs me forward,
Since mine painted the floor.

It is far too easy to play the villain.
I'd gladly fuck your best friend,

Only to leave him wanting
But don't worry, I got my fill.

I would never do as you did,
But I'd be happy to pay forward my pain.

No, I was not made for forgiveness.
You took that from me.

By the Roots

Under a tree,
Down a hill,
You can find
A fairy house

Under pine needle branches.

Iridescent crystal wings,
Half-eaten treats,
And tiny treads
Of unknown feet.

But now
I go to pray
To dead gods
With dry lips,

Cracked from self-loathing,
Whispering harsh words,
Written in a shaky hand
On a post-it note.

Life's Measuring Stick

Sometimes it seems life is measured by pain. Growing pains, skinned knees, and forgotten memories. All of these are measurable. But this pain is by far my favorite to be felt. Not by a cold, sharp knife, or a smooth, warm bottle, but by a smile, a touch, a wish, a kiss, or a promise. This pain is sweet, charmed, easy, and magic. It does not mar but mends, unites, and fulfills. This pain is, quite simply, simple, and it is not pain at all. But it will be measurable.

Between the Lines

I will paint all the flowers a color.
A color bright enough to cover decay.
The decay of a beautiful life drifting to the ground.
The ground will not care what color I pick.
It will only show droplets of the horror I committed.
It is no crime to fall,
But it is to pretend you won't.

From the Four Corners

The wind is a wicked temptress.
The way she plays with your hair
And runs her touch up and down your back.
She teases you into thinking
That all the world loves you.
But the world will never love you.
It will only love what you can do for it,
As a narcissist's play toy.

My Heart

There are times
I just wish I could
Rip my heart from my chest
to watch it beat and bleed,

Only to remind myself
What pain feels like.
What pain looks like.
What life is.

I'm
Just
So
Afraid.

That if I don't,
I will be numb forever.
Plaguing myself with the sins
Of unearned heartache.

You

Somehow you are everything
And nothing that I want you to be.
To be free, yet safe and comfortable.
'Tis a pity that a choice has to be made at all.
Inevitable as it is,
Freedom was not made for
Comfort or safety.

Soon

I feel so strange as of late.
Like soon, I must let something die.
To let something die the saddest death,
That which never had a life to live.
But something stills my hand, my tongue, my lips.
This feels like a dangerous game,
If only to my mind.

Julie Grace

Sometimes

I want to rush
Down rabbit holes of wonderment,
Through doors of lust,
Off cliffs of love,
Only to settle in a garden
Full of falling leaves,
Ripe rose hips
Soaking up the sun's rays,
And steaming cups of tea.
Safe in my own discomfort.
Tormented only by my memories.

Crying

I've always heard,
"Don't cry over spilled milk."
I find that extraordinarily difficult.
What if spilling that milk
Means no pancakes on a Sunday?
How can a week start without pancakes?
If you shouldn't cry over spilled milk,
Can you at least cry over pancakes?

Sunday Afternoons

A good book,
A warm cup of tea,
And a blanket.
Sunshine on your face,
The smell of marigolds,
And breezes from bees' wings
Can cure more than you think.

Longer than Now

With whiskey-kissed lips
And sun-drenched skin
I will wrap myself in the whitest cloth,
Settling down
As the sky turns to sherbet.
I will sit evermore
Waiting to see you bloom.
And then
I will sit even longer
Watching your leaves fall.

One Last Thing

I am inherently uncomfortable
With my own existence.
I wish to float
Hesitantly over my life,
Only offering the suggestion
Of my presence.
Not because I fear I will offend
By existing in completeness,
But because life is all the more delicious
When every touch is just a suggestion.

"Thank you for your consideration. It was a pleasure meeting with you, and I look forward to speaking with you in the future. I think I could be a real asset here."

Printed in the USA
CPSIA information can be obtained
at www.ICGtesting.com
LVHW042255011023
759799LV00066B/541